SUMMARY

OF

BY DAVID GOGGINS

Master Your Mind and Defy the Odds

BY

DEPENDABLE PUBLISHING

COPYRIGHT

This publication is protected under the US Copyright Act of 1976 and other applicable international, federal, state, and local laws. All rights are reserved, including resale rights. You are not allowed to reproduce, transmit or sell this book in parts or in full without the written permission of the publisher. Printed in the USA. Copyright © 2019, by Dependable Publishing.

DISCLAIMER

This book is a summary. It is meant to be a companion, not a replacement, to the original book. Please note that this summary is not authorized, licensed, approved, or endorsed by the author or publisher of the main book. The author of this summary is wholly responsible for the content of this summary and is not associated with the original author or publisher of the main book in any way. If you are looking to purchase a copy of the main book, please visit Amazon's website and search for *"Can't Hurt Me by David Goggins"*.

CONTENTS

CONTENTS 3

CHAPTER 1: WELCOME TO HELL; ESCAPE FROM HELL 5

    KEY TAKEAWAYS 5

    SUMMARY 8

CHAPTER 2: YOU CAN HANDLE THE TRUTH 17

    KEY TAKEAWAYS 17

    SUMMARY 20

CHAPTER 3: NO IMPOSSIBLE TASK. IMPOSSIBLE SPELLS I'M POSSIBLE 25

    KEY TAKEAWAYS 25

    SUMMARY 25

CHAPTER 4: OWNING SOULS 28

    KEY TAKEAWAYS 28

    SUMMARY 29

CHAPTER 5: ALL CALLOUSED UP 36

    KEY TAKEAWAYS 36

    SUMMARY 37

CHAPTER 6: IT'S ALL ABOUT YOUR COOKIE JAR 42

    KEY TAKEAWAYS 42

    SUMMARY 42

CHAPTER 7: YOUR MIND IS THE BATTLEFIELD 45

KEY TAKEAWAYS 45

SUMMARY 45

CHAPTER 8: TALENT IS OVERRATED 48

KEY TAKEAWAYS 48

SUMMARY 49

CHAPTER 9: BEST OF THE BEST 52

KEY TAKEAWAYS 52

SUMMARY 52

CHAPTER 10: FAILURE IS THE UN-TROJAN HORSE 54

KEY TAKEAWAYS 54

SUMMARY 55

CHAPTER 11: WHAT WOULD HAPPEN IF? 60

KEY TAKEAWAYS 60

SUMMARY 60

NOTES 63

CHAPTER 1: WELCOME TO HELL; ESCAPE FROM HELL

KEY TAKEAWAYS

• Growing up, we lived at Paradise Road, Williamsville, Buffalo, New York, an address you could rightly refer to as Hell. Our father, Trunnis Goggins, pretended to our neighbors that all was well with the Goggins family. But it was just a ruse to fool the public.

• If life in that house was Hell, then my father, Trunnis Goggins, was the Devil himself. He abused all of us, my mother, my brother Trunnis Jr., and me, both physically and emotionally.

• My mother, my brother Trunnis Jr., and I, all used to work nights at Skateland (the roller disco that my father owned). I was only 6 years old and my brother only 7 years old, but we both worked at Skateland from 5: PM to about 12 midnight, almost every day. My father paid none of us including my mother who was his cashier.

• At school I couldn't learn anything due to lack of sleep. My young body was often over-stressed, and since I couldn't stay awake at school, it was impossible to learn.

- Also, at school, I was always busy hiding all the bruises I receive from my father's whipping, yet I liked being in school because it was my only safe-place. At school, my father couldn't reach me so I was safe there.

- My father was also a pimp! He usually ran girls across the border to Canada to work in his whore house in Fort Erie. His clientele was mainly men who worked in the Buffalo banking industry. His girls serviced the bankers, so for my father, getting his loan requests approved was never a problem.

- We in the Goggins family were never quick to seek medical assistance because of the Goggins family medical assistance rule. That rule (created and enforced by Trunnis) was as follows: We, the Goggins, do not patronize doctors or dentists. If we became ill or injured, we just shook it off. Never mind that we had no health insurance. Besides Trunnis would never pay for anything that did not directly benefit Trunnis. That was the Goggins family medical assistance rule.

- Life at our house consisted of beat downs, talk downs, more beat downs and more talk downs. Death lingered around our house. It was either going to be my mother first or my father. Many times, my mother planned on murdering Trunnis with Trunnis' own gun but eventually she would relent, knowing full well that eventually it could be her that was going to be murdered first (by Trunnis).

- My mother later hatched an escape plan with the help of Betty, a neighbor who used to live across from us. Eventually, we escaped to my grandparents' home in Brazil, Indiana.

- At Brazil, I repeated second grade at the age of eight. Although I could not read or spell, my second grade teacher, Sister Katherine, a nun, helped me a lot and by the end of the year she had taught me how to read.

- At Brazil, we faced tough and difficult times, mostly financial problems, inability to pay our bills. Trunnis, who made thousands of dollars every night at Skateland, sent us child support of $25 about every three or four weeks. To make ends meet my mother got a job at a department store, and later enrolled us in welfare for the little stipend and food stamps.

- Third grade was unlike second grade! My new teacher, Ms. D, was no Sister Katherine! Ms. D hadn't the faintest patience for a dull student like me. At a point she tried to convince my mother that I ought to be in a school for 'special kids'. I reacted psychologically by developing a stutter.

- The root cause of my problems was that I was suffering from toxic stress brought on by the physical and emotional abuse I had suffered at the hands of my father, Trunnis Goggins. I was clearly a damaged kid.

- So to improve on my performance in tests and to make everyone happy, I started cheating. And lo and behold! I was a good cheat! I cheated at homework, cheated at class work, and cheated during tests and soon my tests scores remarkably improved! Everyone was happy, and the threats of being shipped off to "special education" abated.

- But little did I know that although cheating gave me a momentary reprieve, I was only creating more problems for myself.

SUMMARY

The odds were totally against me as a growing child. Our father, Trunnis Goggins, pretended to our neighbors at the fancy Williamsville, Buffalo neighborhood where we lived that all was well with the Goggins family. But it was all a sham. We lived at Paradise Road, Williamsville, Buffalo, New York, an address you could rightly refer to as Hell.

If life in that house was Hell, then my father, Trunnis Goggins, must have been the Devil because he was both an emotional and physical abuser. He abused all of us (my mother, my brother Trunnis Jr. and I). My father, Trunnis was seventeen years older than my mother, Jackie. And he never married my mother.

In 1981 I was in first grade, but due to lack of sleep, I couldn't learn anything at school. I just couldn't. I and my brother and my mother all worked nights at the roller disco that my father owned. But my father paid none of us (including my mother who was his cashier). He basically took all the money and gave us more work.

My young body was often over-stressed, and since I couldn't stay awake at school, it was impossible to learn. So there really was nothing I could learn at school.

Also, while at school, I was always busy hiding all the bruises I receive from my father's whipping. So I was always trying to stay awake, while trying not to show my bruises, yet I liked being in school because it was my only safe-place, my only get away. At school, my father couldn't reach me so I was safe there and I liked that.

For my mother, living with my father (who never married her) was difficult and painful. So she lived in denial. She pretended as if all was well and carried on as if we were a normal family.

Every day at 6: PM she would make dinner for us at Skateland as if we were all a normal family. But even then, as young as I was, I knew that this was all a façade. It was just all nonsense, all pretenses. We were an abnormal family. Nothing was normal around my father, Trunnis.

One night my mother saw my father sweet-talking a girl at the bar. The girl was one of my father's prostitutes who he usually ran across the border to Canada to work in his whore house in Fort Erie. Yes, my father was also a pimp!

Anyway, my mother knew all this and she also knew that my father had laid up with that prostitute in the past because she caught them in the act. And so when she saw my father sweet-talking the girl, my mother eyeballed my father. My father did not like the public effrontery at all. And of course we all knew that later on, it would come.

Later when we got home that morning around 6: AM, it came. My father, Trunnis, began beating my mother. My mother fought back, but what good could that do. Trunnis was built like a boxer. He grabbed her by the hair and dragged her down the hall. I could see blood coming out of her lip and temple.

At that instant I somehow lost my fear of my father and jumped on his back, slamming and scratching at him and wailing. For a minute, he was surprised at my reaction, and then, of course, he proceeded to beat me black and blue with his belt. In the middle of all this, somehow, my mother managed to activate our house alarm which notified the police, and the police came.

But Trunnis, the sweet talker, sweet talked the cops, buddied up to them and eventually the cops left, smiling and laughing with him, without even interviewing my mother who had activated the alarm and who, obviously, had been assaulted.

One time, my mother who knew I always wanted to be a Boy Scout, signed me up and soon I was scheduled to attend my first Boys Scout meeting. I was so excited. But as we were about to leave for the meeting, Trunnis happened to come home and asked where we were going.

My mother told him she was taking me to my first Boys Scout meeting. He laughed at us and told us we weren't going to any Boys Scout meeting; that instead we were going to the track with him. Of course we didn't want to go to the track. But he forced us to abandon my Boys Scout's meeting and to go to the track with him, anyway.

At the track, Trunnis lost thousands of dollars and was raving as we drove home. At that point I felt so much hate for him that my hate overcame my fear of him and I began to mad-dog him. I told him that we should not have been to the track.

He tried to grab at me but failed, and then he left it alone and just fumed. But of course I knew what was coming. All of us in that car knew what was coming. And later that night it came.

Trunnis beat the hell out of me with his belt, covering my entire body with bruises. But you know what? I did not cry. My hate and anger for him was just too much and it wouldn't allow me to shed a single tear for his satisfaction. I just sucked the pain all up, Spartan like.

One time I had an ear infection, but, of course, my father, Trunnis, would not take me to see a doctor because of the Rule (in addition to the fact that he just didn't care). And my mother, at first, could not either, because she also knew the Goggins Family Medical Assistance Rule.

The Goggins Family Medical Assistance Rule which was, in fact, Trunnis' Rule, was as follows: We, the Goggins, do not patronize doctors or dentists. If we became ill or injured, we just shook it off. Besides Trunnis would not pay for anything that did not directly benefit Trunnis. That was the rule.

And so I suffered with the ear infection until blood began dripping out of my ear. When my mother saw this she became alarmed. The Goggins Family Medical Assistance Rule or not she was taking me to the emergency room (ER). She got me dressed and as we were leaving, Trunnis saw us and asked where we were going. When my mother told him we were going to the emergency room he became infuriated. Standing outside the car while my mother was in the driver's seat, Trunnis tried to wrest control of the car from my mother. Luckily for us, he failed, and my mother quickly sped off with me to the ER.

With us managing to get away, Trunnis went ballistic. He had my brother pour him whisky shot after whisky shot. This, as he berated my brother on why my brother and I should be strong, never soft, and why we shouldn't go off to see a doctor for any little ache and pain, reminding my brother once again that we the Goggins are tough and that we just shake things off.

By the way, according to the ER doctors, we had sought help just at the nick of time. This was because my ear infection had gotten so bad that if we had waited any longer, I was going to permanently lose hearing in my left ear. The fact that I had just narrowly escaped avoidable disability was good news to my mother and me.

But the bad news was that we knew it was coming because we broke the The Goggins Family Medical

Assistance Rule and went to the ER. And as we drove home, silently, from the ER, we knew we were driving closer to it. It was surely coming.

When we got home, it came. And it came in a big way. Simply put, Trunnis Goggins beat the living daylights out of my mother for taking me to the ER. And I'm talking major beat down!

That was our life with Trunnis. Beat downs, talk downs, beat downs, talk downs, and more beat downs and more talk downs.

Death lingered around our house. It was either going to be my mother first or my father. Many times, my mother envisioned murdering Trunnis with Trunnis' own gun but eventually she would relent, knowing full well that eventually it could be her that was going to be murdered first (by Trunnis). It became obvious that she needed to do something drastic (and soon), to escape the oncoming tragedy.

So my mother hatched an escape plan. With the help of Betty, a neighbor who used to live across the street from us, my mother planned to first get herself a credit card, and then escape.

She successfully played Trunnis and got him to cosign for a credit card for her. Eventually she got the credit card (our ticket to freedom). Not long after that she made good our escape from Hell. My mother, my brother Trunnis Jr., and I escaped Hell together.

The Devil tried to chase us in his Corvette, but my mother had anticipated that, and quickly detoured to Betty's house within the city, hiding our car in Betty's garage. The Devil sped off to the highway out of town hoping to catch us on the highway. But in the meantime, we were huddled in Betty's living room within town plotting our next move. We beat the Devil this time!

About eight hours later we arrived Brazil, Indiana at my grandparents' home, and that marked the beginning of the second phase of my life.

At Brazil, I enrolled in a local Catholic school, where I started repeating second grade at the age of eight. At the time, I was practically too dumb to even read or spell. My second grade teacher was a catholic nun, Sister Katherine.

Sister Katherine was the type of teacher who believes every child has his/her own individual learning speed. She never gave up on me. She would take extra time to go over things with me, again and again, just so I could catch up. Before the end of the year she had taught me how to read.

At Brazil, we faced tough and difficult times. Leaving Trunnis Goggins didn't just make our troubles go away. We went through the pains of daily survival. We couldn't pay our bills many times and sometimes we nearly starved. Trunnis, who made thousands of dollars every night at Skateland, sent us only $25 in child support, about every three to four weeks.

My mother got a job at a department store, but her earnings could barely do much for us. Eventually my mother enrolled us in welfare from where we would get a little cash plus food stamps.

My brother, Trunnis Jr., just couldn't adjust to our new life in Brazil and after only a few months, he returned to Buffalo and went back to working for Trunnis at Skateland. After Trunnis Jr. left, my mother missed him so much. But she was also happy that I was coping very well in Brazil, Indiana.

Third grade hit me like a thunder bolt! My new teacher, Ms. D, was no Sister Katherine! Ms. D hadn't the faintest patience for a dull student like me. At a point she tried to convince my mother that I ought to be in a school for "special kids", that is, kids with special learning needs.

The fact that I was now even being considered to be a "special" student tore at me so deeply, bringing on an overwhelming sense of low self esteem. So I was not normal like the other kids? A stigma that would last a life time! All that was too much for me and I reacted psychologically by developing a stutter.

Ms. D could not empathize with me at all. Instead she became even more frustrated and would usually vent her frustration by yelling at me (sometimes, with her face inches away from my face). At a point, the school principal even recommended that I enroll for sessions with a speech therapist, and a psychologist as a condition for my continued enrollment in the school.

School that had once been a safe zone for me; school that had once protected me from Trunnis Goggins in Buffalo, New York, had now suddenly become a slaughter house for my happiness and self esteem, in Brazil, Indiana.

At a stage my stutter got worse. I was later diagnosed with ADHD and prescribed Ritalin (which I did not take). The root cause of my problems was that I was suffering from toxic stress brought on by the physical and emotional abuse that I had suffered at the hands of my father, Trunnis Goggins.

I was clearly a damaged kid. And my performance at school work wasn't getting any better. The threat of being banished to special education still hung over my head like a dark cloud. I needed to do something fast or I would be branded a "special kid" for life.

So in order to improve on my performance in tests and to make everyone happy, I started cheating. And lo and behold! I was good at it! I was a good cheat! So I cheated at homework, cheated at class work, cheated during tests and soon my tests scores remarkably improved! That placated everyone and soon the threats of "special education" abated.

Although my cheating got the "special education" hounds off my neck, it never occurred to me that I was only creating more problems for myself.

CHAPTER 2: YOU CAN HANDLE THE TRUTH

KEY TAKEAWAYS

- When my mum met Wilmoth Irvin, things became different. With Wilmoth in our lives, we felt some support and most importantly, my mother was very happy.

- Wilmoth Irvin was my mum's world, her restoration, her new beginning. Wilmoth was also very cool with me. He was like a father figure to me. But all this was short-lived. Wilmoth was found dead, shot to death in his own house by assassins.

- Wilmoth's death reawakened in me memories of an accident I had witnessed about one year prior. It involved a certain six year old boy who was crushed to death by our school bus while the boy was trying to run to the bus to bring a platter of cookies (presents) to the bus driver. That boy's death gave me the shock of my life.

- After Wilmoth's burial, my mother decided that we would move to Indianapolis. So we moved to Indianapolis.

- At Indianapolis, my mum first enrolled me at the Cathedral High School. Later I switched to North

Central High School. But when my mum came home one day and saw me with a group of gang bangers in her apartment, she moved us back to Brazil, Indiana.

- So we moved back to Brazil. But now, something had definitely changed about Brazil since we moved out to Indianapolis. Racism had become real, aggressive and in-your-face in Brazil.

- One time, my cousin Damien and I were called "niggers", and I had a pistol pointed at my head by one of three rednecks who accosted us as we walked down one country road, on our way home, minding our business.

- Another time the father of a girl, Pam, a brunette I was sitting with at a Pizza Hut barged into the place and warned her never to sit with "this nigger" (me) again.

- There was also an incident in which someone drew (in my workbook) an image of me with a noose around my neck, with the inscription "Niger we're gonna kill you!" written below the drawing. When I reported the incident to the principal, the only thing that caught his interest was the wrong spelling of the word 'nigger'.

- And at Northview High School, I went from cheating in examinations to the forging of results. I would alter my results, changing Fs to Bs and Ds to Cs, snickering at the thought of fooling my mother with the altered results.

- When I realized I had no chance at scholarship to play college basketball, I decided to join the Air Force. I went for the Pararescue Jump orientation course but I didn't qualify. I also struggled with the Arms Service Vocational Aptitude Battery test (ASVAB).

- One evening, I stood in the bathroom, faced the bathroom mirror and called myself to account for all my shortcomings. This later became a habit that helped me to change my life. I would stand in front of the "Accountability Mirror" and call myself out, question myself, caution myself and make restitutions.

- The point is this. Take responsibility for your actions and inactions. Realize that no one is going to change you or care about you as much as you. Be honest with yourself and face reality. Regardless of your past, your future is in your hands, and you have the power to make it whatever you want it to be. Don't ever give up. Keep on fighting.

- Create and use your own "Accountability Mirror". Push the truth up front to your own face. The truth about you might be ugly, but it's your truth. So embrace it and tangle with it and try your best to change it, to change you. It's your truth. And believe it or not (actually believe it!), you can handle the truth.

SUMMARY

When my mum met Wilmoth Irvin (a carpenter/general contractor), we all had a reason to smile. Before Wilmoth all I had ever known was misery and suffering. But things were different now. Wilmoth was laid back and easy going. He was not violent. With him in our lives, we felt some support and most importantly, my mother was very happy.

Wilmoth lived in Indianapolis and he and my mother had plans that we would move to Indianapolis during the summer. Indeed, Wilmoth Irvin was my mum's world, her restoration, her new beginning. Wilmoth and I played basketball together and he was very cool with me. He was like a father figure to me and he was always there. But all this was short-lived.

Wilmoth was soon found dead, shot to death in his own house by assassins. There were talks about shady deals or a drug deal gone bad, we weren't sure. But Wilmoth was sure gone. My mother and I even saw his body being wheeled out of his garage on a gurney and his dried blood splattered, caked, on his driveway. So my mum's world, once again, came crashing down.

Dear life, is this all you are made of? Misery, suffering, and pain? What a life! But, life goes on, right? So we had to move on. And that we did.

Wilmoth's death reawakened in me memories of an accident I had witnessed about one year prior. It involved a certain six year old boy who was crushed to death by our school bus while the boy was trying to run to the bus to bring a platter of cookies (presents) to the bus driver. The boy with a platter of cookies and the way he died gave me the shock of my life.

We were in the school bus. His mum had just dropped him off with his platter of cookies to come join the school bus. But unknown to the bus driver, the boy had stepped in front of the bus. And as the bus jerked forward, it crushed and killed the boy instantly.

I saw the boy in death. I saw his head that had been crushed, flattened like paper under the bus. I saw his brains that had mixed up with his blood. It was a terrible sight that I couldn't just erase from my memory. That boy may have had all the love, attention and support in the world, but he didn't get to see the future.

Somehow, strangely, Wilmoth's death flooded me with memories of the death of the boy with a platter of cookies. I thought about the boy and his death all the time.

After Wilmoth's burial, my mother decided that we would move to Indianapolis, anyway. So we moved to Indianapolis.

At Indianapolis, I had to change schools multiple times. Mum first enrolled me at the Cathedral High School, but as time passed she realized that she couldn't afford it. The tuition was just too high. So, I had to switch to North Central High School (population: 4000 kids), a black community school, where I started hanging out with gang bangers. My mum came home one day and saw me with a group of gang bangers in her apartment. Knowing that she didn't want that kind of life for her boy, she moved us back to Brazil, Indiana.

So we moved back to Brazil. The third school I switched to (this time in Brazil), was Northview High School. At Northview, my schooling high point was my basketball, but I couldn't qualify for college basketball tryouts.

But now, something had definitely changed about Brazil since we moved out to Indianapolis. Racism had become real, aggressive and in-your-face in Brazil. Not that racism was never in Brazil before this. It was. It's just that this time around it had a different attitude. It had stepped out of the shadows and was menacing the community, openly, eager to start incidents everywhere and every time.

Two incidents stick out in my mind. The first was when my cousin Damien and I were called "niggers", and I had a pistol pointed at my head by one of three rough rednecks who accosted us as we walked down one country road in Brazil, on our way home, minding our business.

The second incident happened one time I was hanging out with some girls at Pizza Hut, including one particular Pam, a brunette, that I liked. Soon Pam's father arrived to take her home and saw the two of us sitting together. I could never forget how Pam's father barged into the place and warned her in such a loud voice to never again sit with "this nigger" (me). The place was crowded when this happened and so the embarrassment and humiliation sank so deep.

There was also a third incident. Once in Spanish class, someone drew (in my workbook) an image of me with a noose around my neck, with the inscription "Niger we're gonna kill you!" written below the drawing.

I went to principal Kirk Freeman, and the only thing he could say was... "David, this is sheer ignorance, they don't even know how to spell nigger". I was really disturbed that the only thing that caught his interest was the wrong spelling of the word 'nigger'.

And at Northview High School, I went from cheating in examinations to the forging of results. I would alter my results, changing Fs to Bs and Ds to Cs, snickering at the thought of fooling my mother with the altered results. But my mum (who by then was working many jobs at the same time) never had the time to even ask me for my results. So it really didn't matter whether I was doing well in school or not.

But one day, my results came in the mail to the house. My mum opened the mail and the glory of my real results was all there, in that envelope, for her to behold! That day my mum discovered how badly my school performance was.

I realized I had no chance at scholarship to play college basketball, so I decided to join the Air Force. I went for the Pararescue Jump orientation course but I didn't qualify. I also struggled with the Arms Service Vocational Aptitude Battery test (ASVAB).

At one point my life seemed like one whole big mess. I remember standing in the bathroom, one evening, facing the bathroom mirror and calling myself to account for all my shortcomings. It became a habit that helped me to change my life. I would stand in front of what I now called the "Accountability Mirror" and call myself out, question myself, caution myself and make restitutions.

The point is that, I took responsibility for my actions and inactions. I realized that no one was going to change me or care about me as much as me. I realized that I needed to be honest with myself; that I needed to face reality; and that regardless of my past, my future was in my hands, and that I have the power to make it whatever I wanted it to be. I realized that I should never give up, that I should keep on fighting.

Standing before that Accountability Mirror I would push the truth up front to my face. Often it was ugly. The truth about me was ugly, but it was my truth. So I embraced it and tangled with it and tried my best to change it, to change me. It was my truth. It was ugly. But I learnt that I can handle the truth. I also realized that everybody, even you can handle the truth.

CHAPTER 3: NO IMPOSSIBLE TASK. IMPOSSIBLE SPELLS I'M POSSIBLE

KEY TAKEAWAYS

- My sorry self; a pest exterminator without purpose with a weight of about 300 pounds.

- My struggles with swimming to qualify. I resented my class mates for finding it easy while I struggled.

- The SEALS.

SUMMARY

I was an exterminator, hired by most restaurants in Indianapolis. My job was usually performed at night. It was a demoted life. From the hard core training of a potential Air force service man to becoming an exterminator that set traps for cockroaches and mice, not too much to be proud about.

I became depressed. I dulled my depression with food; milk shakes, half-a-dozen eggs and steak. I became over weight. That night at one of the restaurants where I killed roaches and mice, I knew that the life I was living wasn't what I wanted. And I wanted out.

That clip/ documentary on the US Navy SEALS changed everything for me. Suddenly I knew where I wanted to be. I couldn't get that TV clip about the SEALS off my mind. And, to me that was the beginning of the rest. I started preparing. I started jugging and cycling. I remember even going to the one of the local swimming pools to master my swimming.

I became obsessed with the Navy SEALS. I found myself calling 'active duty recruiters' all over the country. I was ready to move out of state so long as they could get me into the SEALS training. All of them turned me down. That is, until I called petty officer Steven Schaljo. Schaljo asked me to come and gave me a chance even as I weighed 297 pounds. Besides I was the only black when I went there.

To able to get into the Navy SEALS, you have to pass the Arms Service Vocational Aptitude Battery test. I struggled with determination, and studied for hours. When I went for the test, I scored only 44% in the mechanical section of the test, but the requirement for Navy SEALS is 50% for that section. Failing ASVAB made me feel again as though nothing good could come out of me.

It was Officer Schaljo who gave me moral support; as I would call his office sometimes at night, knowing that he would be there. So, I had to prepare again to retake the test. After putting in several hours a day, for the second time, I finally passed, scoring 65% on the mechanical section. My joy knew no bounds.

After celebrating my victory; I went into training. I tried to master my swimming, I ran under cold icy weather when the trees had become naked and icicles hung from roof tops like ice crystals. I swarm in nearly frozen water. That was how determined I was to reshape my life, to make something out of my life.

CHAPTER 4: OWNING SOULS

KEY TAKEAWAYS

- Hell Week was another world. It was where you finally found out if you were made tough. You had to callous your heart because Hell Week is characterized by intense pain and endurance all the way.

- Almost immediately, Psycho Pete transformed himself into my enemy No. 1. He became a thorn in my flesh. He once assured me that I couldn't make it, that I was going to break and leave.

- Hell week involved intense physical pain. But the truth is that it was one big mind game to see how tough in mind you were, to separate the tough minds from the weak minds.

- Unfortunately I was rotated off SEAL Class 230 because I came down with double pneumonia. I didn't quit SEAL Class 230. I was pulled out for medical reasons. Later I joined SEAL Class 231.

- I led my boat crew, Boat Crew Two, in SEAL CLASS 231. I was positioned up front, from where I provided moral support and motivation to my crew. I made sure that my team members why measuring up.

- Hell Week was torture. And of course Psycho Pete and the instructors were watching like eagles, searching for signs of weakness. But I deployed the "owning souls" strategy to get my team to measure up.

- Owning souls is a strategy for winning that involves recognizing that you have a reserve power and that you can call on that reserve power at critical junctures to carry you to victory. It is about putting out your best. It is an internal game. A game you play within yourself. It simply means gaining a tactical advantage for yourself, and if necessary, putting up a defiant act that will nonetheless empower you.

- As Hell Week winded down, it was a special gift to me to see the disappointment on Psycho Pete's face when he realized that I wasn't breaking. Hell Week is designed to break your mind, to see if you'd quit. But if your mind can't be broken, it'd be difficult for you to give up. To quit, first, you need a broken mind.

SUMMARY

Hell Week was another world. It was where you finally found out if you were made tough. You had to callous your heart because Hell Week is characterized by intense pain and endurance all the way.

And, Hell Week started unannounced (well sort of, because the grenade explosion sure did announce it). But here's how it played out. We were all sitting, just chilling in the common room when the first grenade exploded, then almost immediately Psycho Pete blasted through our peace and enjoyment, screaming like a monster, face all swollen, his whole body shaking, exhorting us to get up outta there and get out!

Menacing sounds of heavy machine gun fire rent the night sky in a mad staccato, as incredibly loud grenade explosions intermittently boomed angrily, threatening the night sky with the ferocity of lightning and the audacity of thunder. God! Hell Week had just begun!

And almost immediately, Psycho Pete transformed himself into my enemy No. 1. He became a thorn in my flesh and a mental bully. He once assured me that I couldn't make it, that I was going to break and leave. I was worried about that because he didn't spit and yell it out maniacally like he characteristically did. No Sir! He said it calmly, quietly, and matter-of-factly. Actually, it was better when he screamed at you as usual than when he talks all calm like that. That meant he meant it. And that meant you better take note. So, that got me worried.

Hell week involved intense physical pain. But the truth is that it was one big mind game to see how tough in mind you were. It was all about mind games designed to separate the tough minds from the weak minds. Of course physical endurance came with the territory because a tough mind is the main requirement to achieve physical endurance.

I realized that Psycho Pete tries to mess with your mind every chance he had, in a bid to see how much you can take and if possible break you (but that was the whole point of Hell Week). But, then I also realized that mind games can also work in your favor if you employed them on yourself to help you achieve a task.

I turned Psycho Pete's game against him. Everything he threw at me I absorbed. Through thick and pain and sweat and blood; through the cold freezing water and the yelling and the threats I stood my ground. But unfortunately soon I was rotated off SEAL team 230 because I came down with double pneumonia. I tried like so much to stay put, to hang in there, but they rotated me out of SEAL team 230 to start afresh with SEAL team 231. Well, I didn't quit SEAL 230. I was pulled out for medical reasons. So not much I could do about that.

I wasn't quite healed when the BUD/S class for SEAL Class 231 started, but I had major advantages having been through some of the evolutions before, so I was prepared.

I wanted to be a Navy SEAL, but more importantly, I wanted to be the best. This showed in my zeal and determination. So right from the beginning, I led my boat crew, Boat Crew Two. The toughest and strongest in the crew usually stayed in the front row of the boat. Freak Brown and I were positioned up front, from where I provided moral support and motivation to my crew. Sometimes with looks, or sometimes with just a few words, I nevertheless made sure that my team members why measuring up.

Of course, Psycho Pete was there to make sure things didn't go as easy as we would want them to. And he had been paying a little too much attention to me since I rotate off Class 230 to Class 231. I knew what he wanted. He wanted me to give up, to quit, so that his prophecy could come true. So I became determined not to ever give him that satisfaction. I pushed myself. When others shivered in the cold, I didn't even twitch one bit. When asked to do a rep, I added one extra on top. When others showed exhaustion, I bristled with energy and enthusiasm. And I could see that all of this bothered Psycho Pete.

One day, unexpectedly Psycho Peter decided to extend our 1 mile run to 4 miles. He was leading the run and he quickened his pace. Some boat crews fell back, but not my boat crew. I would not let them. I knew what Psycho Pete was up to. He tried to out run us, but we determinedly stuck on him like white on rice. He would abruptly change the cadence of his run. He would run, then suddenly sprint, then suddenly slow, then suddenly, walk-run, then suddenly jog, then suddenly sprint off again as if the vey hounds of hell were on his heels. And through all this, as exhausted as we were, we stayed on him, literarily clipping his heels. We knew what he wanted. I knew what he wanted. But would not give it to him.

Hell Week was torture, unrelenting, unforgiving, mediaeval torture. It was one evolution after another, one drill after another, torture after torture after torture. And by Wednesday, every cell in our bodies had had enough, but we wouldn't let go. Even when we were doing simple boat raises we were basically dragging ourselves. At that point it was mind over matter.

And of course Psycho Pete and the instructors were watching like eagles, searching for signs of weakness. I hated Psycho Pete and all the other instructors at this point. And I decided that even in our misery, I was going to get Boat Crew Two to show them what they had never seen. Despite that we were practically almost dead with exhaustion, I gingered my team mates, exhorted them to give those instructors a show. Specifically I told them that we should throw our boats as high as ever, and grab it as low as ever, and put up a show. And we did just that to the utter mortification of the instructors. And as we threw the boat up like paper, we even sang along to our rhythm. The instructors were shocked beyond belief. This was straight up superhuman! From where did we muster up the energy, the enthusiasm, the will, the strength? That was the beginning of my "taking souls"/ owning souls strategy.

Owning souls is a strategy I devised for winning, and which you too can deploy to win competitions or take down any obstacles you face in life. It involves recognizing that you have a reserve power and that you can call on that reserve power at critical junctures to carry you to victory. It is about putting out your best. It is an internal game. A game you play within yourself.

Your adversary doesn't even need to know that you are playing this game. Owning someone's soul (as gory as it may sound) does not really involve much of the third party. It simply means gaining a tactical advantage for yourself, and if necessary, putting up a defiant act that will nonetheless empower you.

But note that outward defiance is not always the best strategy. Sometimes you must fall in line even if it is only outwardly (while maintaining your internal defiance). It will depend on your environment, your circumstances. And you must do your homework and be thoroughly knowledgeable about your terrain.

To own souls in battle requires that you prepare your mind and body for battle. It requires that you take an inventory of your strengths and weaknesses; and that you disempower your adversary by magnifying and parading your weaknesses even more than they do, (much to their chagrin).

To own your adversary's soul requires that you act like you're actually helping your adversary to defeat you, while yet maintaining your internal defiance. This will perplex, confound and confuse your adversary. At that point you have owned your adversary's soul. They now belong to you.

To own your adversary's soul, you need to get your game together head of time. You need to research. You need o be knowledgeable about the environment, about your adversary and his/her resources, and about yourself. You need to rehearse, practice, and use your imagination to prepare for different scenarios.

Owning souls does not suppose that difficulties will not arise. They may. But never forget that all difficult situations are finite! They always eventually come to an end. So remember that difficulties are ultimately temporary. An end to them will eventually come. So persevere and you will win.

Anyway, after that show, Psycho Pete doubled up on me. He even started taking me one on one for private, personal torture sessions, meant for me alone. One time while everyone slept he marched me down to the beach and had me surfing the cold ocean alone, tired, sleepy, but not broken because I got through that one too.

Another time when I went for medicals for my knee, I came back to the shore to discover that my team was already far out to sea on paddling drill. SBG, one of the instructors threw me a life jacket and told me to swim out to sea and find my team. I dove into the icy water. My crew did not even know that I was coming against them in the cold, turbulent, wavy ocean. Worse was that I was wearing my boots and my knee was wounded. The boot felt heavy like dead weight on my feet. I was struggling to stay afloat, determined to complete the task. Luckily for me, my boat crew heard my calls over the sounds of waves, and pulled me out of the water and into the boat.

As Hell Week winded down, it was a special gift to me to see the disappointment on Psycho Pete's face when he realized that I wasn't breaking. Sometimes, people want to see you fail and they may deploy every tactic to ensure that you fail. But, the moment they realize that whatever is happening around you is not breaking you mentally, and psychologically, they give up. It's all a mind game. Hell Week is designed to break your mind to see if you'd quit. But if your mind can't be broken it'd be difficult for you to give up. To quit, first, you need a broken mind.

By the end of hell week, I had sustained all manner of sores and injuries. I had a swollen knee and knee pains that didn't want to go down. I even had to use crutches at a point. Nevertheless, I still was able to survive Hell Week.

CHAPTER 5: ALL CALLOUSED UP

KEY TAKEAWAYS

- The surprisingly difficult part about Hell Week for me was the underwater knot-tying. The evolutions were no joke, as Psycho Pete wanted me to break at all costs. My feigning strength after each painful evolution made Psycho Pete very disappointed. I knew that my mind had overcome his. That energized me.

- The human mind is capable of more than we can ever imagine. It is capable of doing so much if we master it.

- The more you work on your mind and emotions to defeat your oppressor or the abuser, the more your mind becomes calloused and thick-skinned such that you are able to rise above your abuser's abuses.

- Soon it became apparent that my body had taken too much damage. I could barely walk. X-rays showed a fractured knee cap. I was treated, then told to go home to heal. I didn't quit. I was being sent home to heal. And since I didn't quit I was given a chance to return after healing, but then, I would have to repeat Hell Week for the second time.

- I went home depressed. Met up again with my ex-wife Pam (I was divorced by then). Later Pam told me she was pregnant. This was not quite good news! I knew full well that I didn't love Pam enough to want to spend the rest of my life with her.

- Eventually I went back for BUD/S training, Class 235. I was willing to die than quit the BUD/S. Besides I had already been told that this would be my last chance at it. So I was not smiling at all. I pushed my body to the absolute limit. Pain was my best friend.

- Physical pain strengthens your mind for life's challenges.

- I finally made it through Hell Week and months later I graduated as a Navy SEAL. My mother was at my graduation and she was so happy for me.

SUMMARY

Even with a swollen knee that refused to subside and the constant bouts of coughs that had me coughing up brown mucus, I still saw myself as just a beaten up BUD/SEALS student that was just fine.

The doctor knew I wasn't fine, but I wouldn't show any signs of weakness by telling him how bad I felt. The pain was agonizing, combined with the pneumonia I had. With Motrin for my knee and the some other medications the doctor prescribed for my lungs, the congestion reduced. But even at that, I still couldn't bend my right leg properly. And this obviously screamed trouble.

The difficult part about Hell Week that got me really hit was the underwater knot tying. Staying steady in the water and tying a square knot, that was a big deal for me, especially with my bad knee.

For the knot-tying drill, every BUD/SEAL student is assigned an instructor, and Psycho Pete specifically recommended me for himself.

The knot tying evolutions were no joke, as Psycho Pete wanted me to break at all costs. He would scream "tie me a square knot and the bowline"

Then I would gulp air, go underwater, tie the square knot, and then the bowline. After tying the knots I would come above water, look at my instructor and smile, instead of displaying any signs of physical pains.

My feigning strength after a painful evolution made Psycho Pete very disappointed. After I smiled, knowing that my mind had overcome his, I would suddenly become energized.

In Indiana, when I wasn't used to iron bars of the gym, my palms easily got bruised with sores after I strained to go further in pushups. But after continuous practice in the gym, my hands and palms became calloused, and I could do many pushups even with sores on my palms.

The same principle applies to abuse and all forms of life's hardships. The more you work on your mind and emotions to defeat your oppressor or the abuser, the more your mind becomes calloused and thick-skinned such that you are able to rise above your abuser's abuses.

Failing to qualify for the Pararescue Jump Orientation course broke me. Being left behind and not graduating was a mighty failure for me. But all that feeling of loss and failure was washed away after BUD/SEAL's Hell Week.

Hell Week made me feel special and it gave me a sense of fulfillment and achievement. But it was not enough fulfillment to make me want to quit. The feeling it gave me was the more reason I couldn't stand quitting at all.

Most times in Physical Training (PT) the only thing that got me going was my mind. The mind is capable of doing so much if we master it. My right leg became a serious problem. I couldn't walk effectively with it;

At one point during an underwater evolution, I could feel my right leg tearing into a million pieces and the shock waves of pain that came with it were incredibly deep. No matter how profound my determination, it just couldn't heal a broken bone.

One day, coming back from a mile-long hike back to base, all the damage that had happened to my body was apparent. I couldn't even walk. Yet I had multiple evolutions, trainings and evaluations lined up for me in the weeks ahead. Yet I could barely walk, I was limping. So I limped to medical.

X-rays showed a fractured knee cap. I knew this was very bad news for my future. I was eventually asked to go home to heal. But on getting to the barracks and meeting those who had quit, my stomach sank. Being there with those that had quit half-way made me feel bad, even though I didn't exactly quit. I was being sent home to heal (medical reasons).

I was asked to go home to recover, but since I didn't quit I was given a chance to come back after I finally healed. But coming back means I couldn't continue from where I stopped. This is because class 231 would have passed that phase of the BUD/SEAL training. So in reality it meant I might have to start Hell Week all over again. So that would make the second time I would be rolled back to Hell Week.

I went home depressed. The first person who was waiting for me at the train station was my ex-wife Pam (I was divorced by then). Soon we got back into old habits. Anyway, I was busy preparing my mind to go back to BUD/S training, Class 235, when Pam told me she was pregnant. This was not quite good news! I knew full well that I didn't love Pam enough to want to spend the rest of my life with her.

Even as time was fast approaching for the next class of BUD/SEAL to start, I still hadn't fully healed. But when time came, I went anyway.

It was torture as usual but my mind was way too calloused by that time. I was willing to die than quit the BUD/S. Besides I had already been told that this would be my last chance at it. So if I had another disabling injury that would be it for me. I would be sent home permanently.

So I was not smiling at all. I pushed my body to the absolute limit. I looked pain in the eye and scoffed at it. At a point I had two broken legs but I still ran miles with them, most times in mind-searing pain, but I didn't care. This was my third and last chance, and make it, I must!

The story ended well because I finally made it through Hell Week and months later I graduated as a

Navy SEAL. My mother was at my graduation and she was so happy for me.

CHAPTER 6: IT'S ALL ABOUT YOUR COOKIE JAR

KEY TAKEAWAYS

•	SBG's story about a band of Vikings raiding a village made me realize that truly "the only easy day was yesterday".

•	Even as I maintained 5th position on the track, and waves of exhaustion washed over me; I knew I couldn't stop for a second to rest.

•	I realized that 'Bad water' wasn't about any other thing but me pushing myself to know how much I could possibly achieve in pain.

•	My cookie jar mindset was my energy bank and I utilized it in times of extreme fatigue.

SUMMARY

One day, after a difficult day's work of intense training, SBG came to me and told me about the Vikings. According him, the Vikings were always prepared before a raid. They didn't go partying. They were always prepared.

SBG was a big moral support to me. He wanted me to push more and more, and from experience, I realized that that was the best advice anybody could give you at the time. Even when you think you have succeeded, don't get too flattered by your little success. Keep on pushing or you may be shocked to find out that the same height you attained which you thought was the highest, had become a mere mediocre achievement. But by then you would realize that you never pushed yourself hard enough!

So that night I hit the gym with SBG, him being a veteran, I had no reason to ever doubt him, and till today I am grateful for the fact that I never doubted him.

Bad Water was something more than just a run. It was somewhat like a life achievement. Several times I found myself on the 5th position on track, tired, exhausted with bruised toes, and toenails removed. But still I knew I couldn't afford to relent in the race for a second, I couldn't afford to rest.

This whole thing was not about the trophy. I realized to me it was about defeating my past that was filled with abuse, failure, low self esteem and shame. Each time I pushed harder I won a battle within me. So, I kept pushing and pushing, harder and harder, winning the fight against myself doubt and mediocrity. It wasn't about the trophy any more. There was more to this.

And, there were times when I knew I had to invent ways to keep moving on. That was when I remembered my mum and her jar filled with cookies. I remembered how I was allowed to take one cookie at a time, and I didn't just rush to eat it. I first savored it.

So I employed the "cookie jar" mindset to everything related to physical pain and training. Whenever, I felt I couldn't withstand the pains of exhaustion and fatigue, in my mind's eye, I would dip my hands into my cookie jar and take a piece of cookie. And as I ate this mental cookie I would feel a flood of energy wash through me. That would keep me going and distract me from the present pain.

When faced with the challenges of life, you may want to use this mind trick. The mind can be distracted from pain. You only feel pain because your mind is focused on it. The moment your mind focuses on something else, that pain will go numb. The mind pays attention to whatever we force its attention to.

If your mind perceives that you care so much about your pain, it will surely focus on your pain and stay on it. But the moment you make your mind feel your pain is less important than the task at hand, your mind will focus on your task and ignore your pain.

CHAPTER 7: YOUR MIND IS THE BATTLEFIELD

KEY TAKEAWAYS

- I knew I had so many weaknesses even while preparing for the Badwater race. But I got over them and forged ahead.

- My mind was my battle field.

- Quitting is usually a premeditated thought. It didn't just happen in an instant.

SUMMARY

I was superfluous with weaknesses, by my own standard, but I didn't allow it get over me. I was ready to use the greatest weapon we have ever known "our minds" to overcome all the weakness that may want to defeat me in the race.

I worked double, pushed my mind, and hurt myself without even knowing it. But at this point I had already gained mastery over my mind and over my body. Failure at this point didn't mean losing the race. Failure to me meant not allowing my physical body to actualize its full potential.

I wanted to stretch as far as I could, knowing that I would not break, I was confident I wasn't gonna break, no matter how much I stretched! I had developed so much faith in myself that I felt everything can be achieved and is attainable with hard work and focus.

Every time I became overwhelmed by the stress and hard work that accompanied success, my mind kept reminding me that I was a nobody. It would come like a mocking voice saying something like:

"Why are you here?"

"You have no place here".

'Please give it up'.

"Why are you causing yourself so much pain?"

"You can leave all this pain and just go home".

But knowing that those were the voices of impending failure ringing in my head, what I did was to make my mind the battle field, taking the war to where the enemy is (my perceived susceptibility for failure). And even when I fought and labored in physical training and those difficult evolutions, I wasn't competing with the other racers anymore, I was fighting myself. It gave me the greatest focus ever.

The focus one achieves when one becomes his own competition is totally powerful. At that point you can't see anyone else but your other self that is meant and designed to be a winner.

My mind being the battle field in times of challenges has made me come this far today. If I were petty enough to always compete with every athlete I met on the track, or to always compete with my class mates in SEALS training, then, my mind would have been perpetually unproductive.

I often tell people that their mind is the greatest weapon they can ever have in life's warfare. Once you can control your mind, it is easy for every other thing to fall into place.

Most people that quit didn't just face a challenge they couldn't surmount and then gave up the fight. Instead quitting was something that had been premeditated over time. Perhaps one challenge or the other they had encountered in the beginning of the quest had already adulterated their faith and since then they had been losing steam. And the more your faith weakens, the harder and intense the slightest challenge would become. Once your mind has already become compromised, even the smallest, slightest challenge would become a huge, insurmountable task for you.

CHAPTER 8: TALENT IS OVERRATED

KEY TAKEAWAYS

• Talent may not be critical for achieving great feats. If talent was the sole requirement, then, nobody would have heard of 'David Goggins'. I followed the principle of hard work. Hard work works.

• I constantly engaged my body in physical tasks that I knew were suppose to be beyond my physical body's limit.

• Gary Wand being the favorite in the race inspired me. It didn't deter me.

• Coming second place to Land Shark was obviously because I lacked backdrops.

• Admiral Ed Winters summoned me, gave me the real shivers, until he unraveled his purpose. He said the Navy was terrible at recruiting African Americans into the Navy SEALS and he wanted me to help the Navy do the recruiting.

• When giving recruitment speeches, I usually used my life's story as the perfect motivator.

- I can't forget the day young that was waiting for at the finish in the race, after I reached the finish line, he said " I drove two hours just to see you finish".

- But of course when you think everything is all fine and dandy, life throws you a curve ball. I was suddenly diagnosed of a hole in the heart. But then, I didn't see it as a stumbling block. I also didn't see myself as an extraordinary person that could do all that I did, even with a hole in the heart. To me all that mattered were "will" and "drive".

SUMMARY

Truly, talent wasn't required in achieving great feats. If talent was the sole requirement, then, nobody would have heard of 'David Goggins'. The basic truth was that I was a fighter. I fought to overcome all the odds that were against me, and there were many! Talent is ruled out in my case. I followed the principle of hard work.

I used to constantly put my body into seriously challenging tasks that I knew were beyond the average. I sweated it out, and most of the time, I blooded it out. I was always bruised.

I knew I didn't have much talent. Even from high school, I was a cheat nearly throughout high school. I lacked the mental balance due to my early childhood abuse. I lacked the intellectual basis to be smart when I was a boy. Everything I can do today was produced from sheer determination to excel against all odds. I knew that if things were different for me as a child, it would have been better, but I never submitted myself to those fantasies and wishes! I accepted myself the way I was, and went all the way for a 'Destiny's U-turn'.

A fellow racer called Gary Wand was an amazing runner and athlete. He was the favorite in the race even before he had reached the finish line. All the reporters were already waiting for to interview him.

Now, for someone that had put in so much outside his physical boundaries, not getting the prized as the winner would have demoralized him, but not me! Just because I was always preoccupied with contesting with myself, I wasn't aware of winning. All I did was put in my all. And, in truth all that ever mattered to me was finishing 'strong'.

Land Shark was another incredible athlete I ran with on track. I didn't prepare enough, and I lacked a basic trick, or rather, I didn't practice a basic trick called 'back drops'.

Backdrops is a skill used in warfare. It is all about understanding the landmark of a terrain and being able to maneuver other routes to arrive at your destination.

Land Shark used that to win. I came second to Land Shark in the race.

When I received a phone call that Admiral Ed Winters wanted to see me, I was taken aback. I started thinking that I may have done something that has embarrassed the Navy SEALS.

The chain of command is usually broken down, so that a junior officer does not communicate directly to highly placed officer, especially one such as an Admiral.

When I got there, I couldn't look at him directly when he spoke and was obviously nervous. Then he broke the ice. He told me that he was impressed with my athletic achievement and my recruitment record.

He went further to talk about the need for more colored people to join the Navy SEALS. He said the Navy was not good at recruiting African Americans into the Navy SEAL and that they needed my help to accomplish that. In fact, it became my new detail. The admiral and I eventually made the first stop together on our recruitment tours.

For my recruitment tours, I used a powerful tactics when giving a speech. I talked about my pathetic early life's story. That usually held my audience spell bound. I talked a lot about not giving up. I would always exhort them to remember Rocky in the boxing movie. He never gave up! That movie "Rocky" was a huge source of inspiration for me and I kept that video cassette for years, knowing its worth to me.

But of course when you think everything is all fine and dandy, life throws you a curve ball. I was suddenly diagnosed of a hole in the heart.

But then, I didn't see it as a stumbling block. I also didn't see myself as an extraordinary person that could do all that I did, even with a hole in the heart. To me all that mattered were "will" and "drive".

CHAPTER 9: BEST OF THE BEST

KEY TAKEAWAYS

• My life was a circle of war and rest. I didn't get involved in the parties SEALS engage in. I lived the life of a Spartan.

• I was a diehard goal getter. My OIC thought I actually wished I was a prisoner of war (so, as just to know if I knew what it takes to last!).

• I put in so much in the Ranger Training, that my OIC had to caution me!

SUMMARY

After training' all I did was rest, preparing my body for tomorrow's challenge. Usually the SEALS socialize. But I was never part of it. My body was too occasioned to war and the next challenge! Just like the Spartans, always ready for war. Not that socialization is bad, but I had to prepare myself for the next challenge so there was no room for socialization. I wasn't ready to give failure the slightest chance to invade my life.

I joined Ranger School. My OIC probably thought I was going overboard with my rare enthusiasm that he once said that he thinks I actually wished that I was a prisoner of war (POW) just so I could test myself to see if I could survive it.

As leader of Physical training (PT) I was ever intensifying physical training. But, then my OIC cautioned me to lay low with my intense regimen. According to him, Ranger Training (RT) wasn't in anyway the Navy SEALS! I lost respect for their leadership immediately, for submitting to mediocrity.

I also trained with the Delta Force. Yes I was everywhere in my quest to prove that I was uncommon even among the uncommon.

CHAPTER 10: FAILURE IS THE UN-TROJAN HORSE

KEY TAKEAWAYS

- I had a second heart surgery which went well. The Navy gave me two years to recuperate and deployed me to recruiting, a non-combat job. I did that for two years.

- After the two years of recuperation, I re-enlisted with Delta. I blazed through Delta Selection. But during one land navigation test I used unapproved roads and broke protocol. I was sent packing. I flunked Delta Selection!

- I tried to break the Guinness world record in pull ups on the Today Show with Matt Lauer, but failed in front of millions of people.

- I attempted (the second time) to break the record again, this time at a Crossfit Gym in Nashville. And I failed again.

- I tried again (the third time) at the Crossfit in Brentwood Hills. I went back to my Hell Week strategy of owning souls and dipping into that cookie jar in my mind. I finally broke the world record with 4030 pull ups!

- Choose your company wisely. Ensure to surround yourself with people who will empower you, not feed you with mediocrity. The war of most challenges and obstacles is fought in the mind. And in the heat of battle, you need a foxhole partner who will feed your courage and purpose, and not one who will talk you out and down into defeat.

- Remember this. Failure is the un-Trojan horse. At first it looks like a bad gift, but take a closer look because inside failure you will see the truths and clues to your success.

- Handle your failure (s) properly. Don't ever allow failure to derail you from your mission. Do not blame other people for your failures, or blame it all on bad luck or circumstances. Do not succumb to doubt. No one is immune to failure and life was never fair to begin with. Just keep at it and you will be victorious in the end.

- After I became the new world record holder I did not celebrate my success. Why? Because I am the proverbial horse chasing after the carrot stick. For me, it was all about the pursuit, the hunt, and not necessarily about the prize or the accomplishment. I am wired that way!

SUMMARY

My second heart surgery went well. I now had a functional heart muscle. But I was in no rush. All I had to do was to recuperate properly. The Navy gave me two years to do that. They deployed me to recruiting, a non-combat job. I did that for two years.

Recruiting gave me the chance to inspire new intakes. I met a lot of people who were like me when I started. I gave them the hope that they badly needed for that stage of their lives. I realized that my not being engaged in combat activities or not being intensely engaged in physical challenge was after all, a phase for me.

In 2011, after the two years of recuperation, Admiral Winters helped me to re-enlist with Delta. Oh yes Delta. I had some business to finish with them! I blazed through Delta Selection like an inferno, crushing tasks here and there.

But during one land navigation test where I was supposed to be checking my map to ensure I was headed in the right direction, I did not do that, and I ended up going off course. I was almost out of bounds! To get back on course and meet my objective, I decided to cheat. I used unapproved roads and broke protocol. I was sent packing. I had just flunked Delta Selection!

I didn't blame fate or circumstances for flunking. I took it as my cross to bear. Even when team mates came to me with encouraging words, I still saw the error and danger in what I did. I took responsibility for my actions. Taking responsibility is an asset!

Going home, I thought to myself, it was another opportunity to work on myself.

I rejoined the SEALS and for the next two years was based in Honolulu.

I tried to break the Guinness world record in pull ups on the Today Show with Matt Lauer, but failed in front of millions of people. But I did not give in to shame.

I attempted breaking the record again, this time at a Crossfit Gym in Nashville. I failed again. My hands, my Achilles heel, gave out on me, thorn to pieces like raw hamburger. I couldn't go on. I had to give up the attempt. I failed again.

But even in the ER, my mother who was with me sized up my wounds and the situation and just said matter-of-factly that I would attempt the record break again. And that was exactly what was on my mind.

And this brings me to an important point. Ensure to surround yourself with people who will tell you what you need, not just what you want. The war of most challenges and obstacles is fought in the mind. That's where you win it, or lose it. And in the heat of battle, when you are hunkered down in a fox hole with your colleague or colleagues, make sure they are of the quality that will empower you, feed your courage and purpose, not talk you out and down into defeat. Choose your company wisely.

In life, failure is the un-Trojan horse. It looks like bad news, like a bad gift, but look again! Upon closer inspection, you will find that inside failure lie the truths, the clues, the elements to success. All you need to do is look with sincerity.

Another thing is that you've got to handle failure appropriately. Don't ever allow failure to derail you from your mission, or mess up your relationships with the people around you. Know that no one is immune to failure and that life was never fair to begin with, anyway. Do not blame other people for your failures, or blame it all on bad luck or circumstances.

Do not succumb to doubt. Just say to yourself that you will overcome your challenge and keep trying. It might take one try or a thousand tries, but determination and perseverance will always trump challenges and "so called" impossibilities any day! Keep at it and you will be victorious in the end.

Two months after I failed at my attempted record break, I was back at the attempt again at the bar at Crossfit in Brentwood Hills. I went back to my Hell Week strategy of owning souls. This time, I needed to own the record holder's (Steve Hyland's) soul.

I mentally positioned him as my mortal enemy from whom I had to retrieve my own very soul that he had taken from me. I fought tooth and nail, dipping in that cookie jar in my mind that opened up for me whenever I need to own a soul. I became a cyborg, an un-human in a steel trance. My very being was possessed by only one thought: to own that soul at that moment. It was either that or nothing!

And it was in this mental state that I finally did 4030 pull ups. And, at long last, the record became mine! Finally!

But even then I did not celebrate my success. In fact, becoming the new world record holder was anti-climactic for me. Why? Well, I had always known the truth, and that was the reason for all my accomplishments so far. I am the proverbial horse chasing after the carrot stick.

The truth is that I can never stop. I will always be on the hunt for the next challenge. For me it was all about the hunt, not necessarily the prize or the accomplishment. So I knew that I would always be in pursuit, on the hunt. I am wired that way. What a life!

CHAPTER 11: WHAT WOULD HAPPEN IF?

KEY TAKEAWAYS

• I was pushing on, against all odds. I was fatigued, dizzy and even when the doctors couldn't ascertain what was going on inside of me, I pushed on. Fear didn't overthrow my sense of purpose. I fought through it.

• All my life I have struggled against and through the odds. From domestic abuse to low self esteem. But, when I took ownership of my life and my fate, I conquered fear and limitations.

• Keying into Joe Hippensteel's stretching techniques; I opened my body for a new self physical therapy. My body became almost born anew.

SUMMARY

Have you ever wanted to relent, to give up, and a small voice asked you the "what would happen if" question? Like, "what would happen if you tried one more time?" This advice goes for positive achievers. "What would happen if" is the ultimate question for that man/woman who is thinking of giving up after supposedly using up all his/her perceived chances in doing whatever. "What would happen if" is the question that gets you to make that next move which might give you your being break!

OK, although my body had become so damaged, I was obviously still pushing on because the "what would happen if" question plagued me. And I felt that if I gave up without trying that next move, I may never ever forgive myself. I was pushing against all odds. And even though fatigue, physical pain, and anxiety breezed through my mind, somehow, I never gave up the fight.

For all the life's struggles I had passed through, I wanted a mental platform from where I could give my challenges a "hard time". I wanted to be in charge of my success. I stopped believing in luck and chance or fate. For what if in fate I had a bad omen. So, I realized that, without much talent, my only prospects for getting what I wanted in life would be by getting it through "the hard way", through hard work! What would happen if I worked harder? What would happen if I gave it another try? What would happen if I gave it one more push, one more pull, one more twist, one more rep, one more word? What would happen if?

This motivated me to borrow a page from Joe Hippensteel book. Joe Hippensteel was an extraordinary athlete who defied his genetic makeup. He was small and his competitors on the track were bigger and faster than him. But he did not let that deter him. He pushed forward and developed his lower body to gain more physical strength there.

But, in constantly doing so, he sustained so many injuries, including a severed hamstring. So he started giving himself physical therapy, his own special stretching exercises. With time he realized that his techniques worked for him. And at a point the Navy even consulted him to train military athletes on the 'stretching technique'.

With my body continually tightening up on me, I tried Joe's stretching techniques and with time mastered it. It worked and gave me a more capable body that was not so much huddled with pain any longer. Today, I understand my body far better because of Joe's stretching techniques, and I have gained more flexibility!

The moral of the above is that you should always look out for second opinions from people who have crossed the same bridge you are struggling to cross. And always ask yourself the achiever's ultimate question.

What would happen if'?

NOTES

NOTES

NOTES

NOTES

RECOMMENDED FOR YOU!

SUMMARY OF STRESS LESS ACCOMPLISH MORE
BOOK BY EMILY FLETCHER
Meditation For Extraordinary Performance

BY
DEPENDABLE PUBLISHING

SUMMARY OF UNDER PRESSURE
BY LISA DAMOUR
CONFRONTING THE EPIDEMIC OF STRESS AND ANXIETY IN GIRLS

BY
DEPENDABLE PUBLISHING

SUMMARY OF THE LIFE-CHANGING MAGIC OF TIDYING UP
BY MARIE KONDO
The Japanese Art of Decluttering and Organizing

BY
DEPENDABLE PUBLISHING

SUMMARY OF MOSTLY SUNNY
BY JANICE DEAN
How I Learned to Keep Smiling Through the Rainiest Days

BY
DEPENDABLE PUBLISHING

SUMMARY OF IT'S NOT SUPPOSED TO BE THIS WAY
BOOK BY LYSA TERKEURST
Finding Unexpected Strength When Disappointments Leave You Shattered

BY
DEPENDABLE PUBLISHING

SUMMARY OF DARE TO LEAD
BOOK BY BRENE BROWN
Brave Work. Tough Conversations. Whole Hearts.

BY
DEPENDABLE PUBLISHING

SUMMARY OF THE GREENPRINT
BOOK BY MARCO BORGES
Plant-Based Diet, Best Body, Better World

BY
DEPENDABLE PUBLISHING

SUMMARY OF THE THEFT OF AMERICA'S SOUL
BY PHIL ROBERTSON
Blowing the Lid Off the Lies That Are Destroying Our Country

BY
Dependable Publishing

SUMMARY OF NEXT LEVEL BASIC
BOOK BY STASSI SCHROEDER
The Definitive Basic Bitch Handbook

BY
DEPENDABLE PUBLISHING